My Eclipsed Star

A tale of grief bigger than the whole sky

by

Colleen Bridget Griffith

Trigger Warnings:

Fertility Treatments*
In Vitro Fertilization (IVF) Treatment*
Pregnancy Loss*
Depression
Anxiety

If you or someone you know is experiencing a mental health crisis, please reach out for help. Call 911: If someone is in immediate danger, call 911. Call 988: Get connected to the National Suicide Prevention Lifeline by dialing 988. Crisis Text Line: Get 24/7 help from the Crisis Text Line.

I would not have been able to get through such a difficult time in my life without the help of my mental health care team made up of professionals in addition to my vast support network of friends and family who reached out. If you are struggling, it's always okay to ask for help.

* These subjects are not typically given a trigger warning, but if you are reading this and have gone through something similar, you understand how triggering and upsetting it can be to be blindsided while trying to enjoy a book, tv show, movie, etc.. I've learned in the past year how complex all the feelings from going through treatment are and this book is my attempt at making sense of them. If you are going through what I did, I feel you deserve the courtesy of a warning before reading.

I know there are many books out there that tell the story of IVF or women going through fertility struggles and they tend to end with a pregnancy. I did not want to have that in this book because I wanted others to know you can heal from this trauma even if that's not how your story ends at the time.

About the Author

Colleen Griffith, also known as The Sassy Blonde Writer, has been writing since she could hold a pencil and dreamed about being a published writer since people started asking her what she wanted to be when she grew up. Never particularly attached to any genre, Colleen documents her journey on her YouTube channel Sassy Blonde Writer as well as her website and Instagram of the same name. When she's not writing, Colleen works as an elementary music teacher.

Works by Colleen Griffith

Children's Books
Prickly Mrs. Pearl

Poetry
My Eclipsed Star (you're reading it now!)

Novels
Cloak of War (forthcoming)

My Eclipsed Star

A tale of grief bigger than the whole sky

by

Colleen Bridget Griffith

"You never arrived in my arms,
but you will never leave my heart."
—Zoe Clark Coates

Contents

INTRODUCTION

The choice to be a poet

I used to think that poetry was

Something I couldn't write

But then you feel something

So intense

It burns

Burns so bright that prose

Or typical storytelling cannot express it

So here it is.

Sad facts and statistics

Do you know how many women have pregnancy loss?
Nearly 10 to 20 percent
But so many suffer in silence
I hope this book will end that trend
Why shouldn't we speak openly about our pain?

Do you know how many women need help to conceive to start their family?
In the United States, more than 55,000 women give birth to a baby conceived through assisted reproductive technologies
The rate for a first-time success
Is 65%
Commonly, the first one doesn't take

The beginnings

When the September gloom cascaded over me,
I refused to let it drown me
I grasped and groped for a lifeline

In October, a new hope appeared in the fog
A faint glimmer
I dropped my baggage and ran toward it

In November and December, we celebrated what
we thought was the end of our journey
On paper, it was over
But the new year came, and January brought a
new shade of gray

Now the skies refuse to be blue
And anguish rages in the sea
The heavens lied and sent me hurt
The earth takes on the anger for me
The fates laughed at my daughter
They mocked me and my wife's pain

But the Gods and Goddesses won't let this go
They used the cards to encourage me to try again
Although I am not ready now,
I refuse to let the fates win
The celestial beings have inspired me

To take my destiny back again.

A message for those who grieve

Take special notice of who reaches out
when you are not okay

Don't hide your pain, let it out
and remember the ones who stay

Not the ones who lurk in the background,
nor the ones who send thoughts and prayers

The ones who stay and listen to you
Are the friends for any weather

Make no excuses for the others,
Who only gawk from afar

Their role in your past doesn't matter now,
Only those who soothe your scars

When people ask if you're okay,
Don't lie and say you're fine

Real friends deserve to know,
And fake ones deserve a goodbye

If they're too afraid of your sadness,
They don't need to stick at your side

Wow you're so strong

Other people tell you how strong you are and ask how you do it, but they aren't satisfied when you say,

"Because I have to."

All the articles say not to beat yourself up afer a failed cycle like it's easy. The guilt and self-loathing seep into you like hot water into a tea bag.

I'm tired of people telling me I'm strong and that what I'm going through is unimaginable. I don't have to imagine it because I lived it. The longing after trying for so long, the anger when the tests came back negative, and the fear that lingered like a monster in the dark depths of the sea that there was something wrong and no one else knew.

THE TRYING

What happens when you start trying (a journey)

What happens when you start trying (a journey) You start your journey of trying to have kids bright-eyed and bushy-tailed and full of all these nice dreams. You follow the guides religiously and you test and you time everything perfectly but, for some reason, it doesn't work.

After 6 months of trying you find yourself starting to lose your mind.

You fret and you toil and you feel like something is wrong because shouldn't it have worked by now and you wish more than anything you could be one of those people who get pregnant the first time they try so this heartbreak you feel would leave you alone, but you know your life was never meant to be that easy. You feel an ache in your heart because you know you are ready to carry your child into the world and hold them through life.

Some people try to make sure you're serious about trying like you don't know or haven't looked up how hard being a parent is. Some people assumed you weren't going to even try because you got a Master's and seemed so focused on your career, which stings in a way you didn't think possible. Are you sure?

Bandwidth haikus

Please do not worry
I can handle all you throw
But those curve balls hurt

Used to being strong
I will forget I can break
Until it's too late

Forgive me for limits
I did not know I had them
I can't take on more

It's hard to admit
But let me apologize
To myself for lying

When it's time to get help

Society tells you to wait a year, but your gut tells you after half a year something is up. You find a clinic where you and your unconventional family feel safe and the care team tests you even more.

They test you and your other half to find out who the problem is. One of you is poked and prodded with catheters impaling your most sensitive parts. The other has two simple tests.

They find that the one thing that made her feel like her true self is also the reason why your last six months have been all for nothing, so now it's time to use the frozen four.

But the place with the samples you froze "just in case" drags its feet, giving you the runaround for months and months on end until you find scissors big enough to slice through their red tape and they finally send the frozen four to their new home.

First loss

The first loss hurt because it was the first real chance. Not only do you find out you're not in that special 20% or 30% who can conceive after this, but you bleed.

You bleed so much it gives you a panic attack at work because, yes, you went to work because stupidly you thought it would be a good distraction, but it's all so trivial you can't bring yourself to care because you can't do this, you can't be a normal person with this much pain.

You call all three of your admin, two who've known you for years but can't be bothered to pick up, one who has known you a week actually gives you the time of day and, thankfully, she's the one who actually helps you and treats you like a human again.

But then you go home and maroon rapids toss you around and you get scared something is terribly wrong.

So, you go back and you get poked and prodded while you're already in immense pain and the weekend man says there's nothing wrong and comments that the procedure should have worked.

You don't know if he meant for it to sound like it's something you did wrong that made it fail, but you feel that way all the same.

A funeral for failure

I felt a funeral in my brain
The call to madness outside

The martyrs all were gawking
At what had ceased to be alive

And though what I had been mourning
Was not something that had properly died

I felt the grief drown and overwhelm me
From what the casket had inside.

The scars from where my heart had shattered
Hide my stolen joy's escape

With witching wails and gnashing teeth
Weakened faith as it failed

And though I know my darling hope
Is not forever lost

I can't help but lay a flower
At the tomb of what I lost.

If at first, you don't succeed, you try IVF

After a weekend of mourning and feeling dead inside and biting the heads off your friends who try to help, you decide with your other doctors at the clinic that, between the limited numbers of samples and the odds that were too painful because you weren't special enough for them to be in your favor, the next best plan is to inject yourself with hormones and feel like a pumpkin patch before they harvest the eggs.

The retrieval

I showed them all how much I love and want you
When they asked me to inject myself
With hormones and drugs that stormed through
    my body
To help create little you
That distorted me and made me ache and feel like
    I was going to be crushed
I balanced my brain
With prescription chemicals from doctors
To tame the anxious beast
That got aggravated by the storm
If there was more I could have done
To keep you in my womb
Please know I would have done anything
To hold you in my arms
We have never heard your voice
Or to know what makes you laugh
But whatever afterlife you end up in
We will search for your path

After the retrieval

For over a month, you feel pain in your ovaries as they puff up and horror at all the bruises from the injections in your stomach.

You thought the changes would make you nastier than ever, but they only made you weep. You feel disgusting to look at.

But then you have the harvest and it comes with such fruitfulness and the little pumpkins from your pumpkin patch do so well that it seems like luck is finally on your side.

You have to wait longer than expected but, after the holiday season and your birthday, you finally go in to transfer your beautiful embryos and all seems well.

The week after, you feel a connection to your baby-to-be, and you and your love feel her aura and energy so strong.

A perfect week of a blissful life. You let yourself think the journey is moving forward.

But then you get the call.

All the prayers and hopes people were sending to you didn't work.

All that you did to manifest didn't work.

Your friends who have never been where you are don't understand as they try to remind you that science just fails sometimes, and you think about how your own magic failed too.

They tell you the odds get better on the second try, but you start to doubt if you should bother going through it all again.

Why should you? Your prayers went unanswered, and your spells didn't work. Why should you waste your time again?

Then you have to wait to bleed, an agonizing thing to know, and wake up with the dread of knowing any day now you're going to lose her.

Any. Day. Now.

Medical, Medical

One of the nurses says to let her know if there is anything she can do and you say, "All I want is my baby but you can't give that to me."

You keep asking the clinic if there's something wrong with you and that's why it didn't work, or if it's because you took that extra strength Tylenol when you were having lower back pain, or because you helped hold up a kindergartener who needed to get on their tippy toes to get a drink from the water fountain, or if you have a hostile uterus and no one knew, or it's just something that happens and there was nothing you could do...

And if you don't bleed does that mean it actually worked or are they going to give you something to induce your period and take her away again?

So you schedule a call with your doctor because the nurses are tired of not knowing how to help you more, and you have to find a nice way to ask her why it didn't work and if there's something wrong with you and that's why it didn't work and what's going happen if you don't bleed because you still haven't. But of course, once you have your meeting you don't need to ask that last one.

It wasn't going to be over until you bled, but it is now.

When the bleeding starts, you wonder, "How can someone bleed so much and not die?"

THE MOURNING

The process

Hope is a thing with feathers
But today it flew away from me

They said to trust the process
But the process didn't trust me

Instead, it searched for my flaws and cracks
And crept away like a thief in the night
Then asked me to forgive it, as if what it did was
right

So now I begin a new process
And that process is called Grief

It has painted my rosy lens grey
And corrals me like its sheep

In the shock I allow it to lead me
But then I come back to myself

The way through it isn't to follow along
The way out is to push through
Before it's the only story you can tell

The day we got the news

Coming home
On the day we learned the news, everything was a
        blur.
First comes the shock of it all, then the disbelief.
                            Then

                            comes

                            the

trying-to-be-normal-for-just-a-

              second-so-I-can-go-on-autopilot-

                                    and-not-use-
my-brain
so I can figure out my next feeling about...this.

Then in the shower, as I'm trying to wash the
rest of the day off, it really hits me.
Through the pelts of water
I wail and scream and sob—I can't feel her like I
        used to.

The second day followed...

The third, the shock of horror

The fourth day, it got better, and we felt almost

human again. Our inner wounds started to scab over. But then came the physical pain just for me.

Why is destroying so much faster than building? Two days to undo two weeks of progress

Five days later...
I'm getting good at pretending I'm not sad all the
        time
But when people talk about what there is to
        celebrate, I have no words.
Honestly, I don't think I'm going to be able to have a good time like I used to, but I'm going to try to just not be sad.

I was fine until after the tarot readings when a friend asked when we were going to meet Angela Amanda, and Dewy said, "We tried, that's why this week has been so tough," or something along
        those lines.
I went to the bathroom because it was too painful for me to talk about.

When I came back, I was like "Are we done being
        sad? We're gonna go party?"

But while we were out, I kept thinking about how sad I was and worrying whether Angela Amanda would want us to be out instead of inside mourning her, and how tomorrow when I see my mom I'm going to fall apart and say "Mommy, I lost my baby. Why did I lose her? It's not fair."

And she's going to say, "I don't know honey" just like the doctors and nurses and Google.

Today, I shed my sadness like a snake. At least,
      I hope...

Six days later
My sadness kept seeping into my soul while we
were out dancing.

Maybe because it was something I wanted to
share with my little girl, how much I love to
dance, or because it's something I'll never get
to do with her, or maybe because, just before
we went out dancing, a well–intentioned friend
couldn't read the room and asked why we kept
the candle going next to a jar of stars that said
her name.

Whatever the reason, I wanted to lose myself
more than usual on the dance floor.
The fog from the machines was perfect because it
hid my melancholy face.
But then my mom came back and shared all the
outpours of love she had received for me.
A narrow escape from insanity and my own self–
pity

Every day after

Ten Questions for care team:

1. Why did you let me think this would work?

2. Why didn't you tell me not to give her a name?

3. Why didn't you tell me not to call her my daughter?

4. What am I supposed to do with all this love I was ready to give her?

5. Why wasn't there a warning that if it doesn't work l would infect everything I touch with sadness?

6. Why did that one male doctor who I saw after the IUI didn't work tell me it should have worked like there was something wrong with me and put that horrible thought in my head?

7. Is there something wrong with me?

8. Was there something I did wrong after the treatment?

9. What was I supposed to do to make it work?

10. Why is the only way to talk to you and get answers about this horrible thing to talk on the phone like it's easy to talk about out loud?

Why I hate the wheel

The Wheel of Fortune mocked and teased
I drew it four times in two days before
The news that nearly ended me
I thought it was a sign of luck, but it was of
circumstances unseen
And for that betrayal of my trust, I do not trust its
uncertainty

Luck that is good or bad depends on how you flip
the coin
Depending on the journey you take, it could lead
to death or two lovers joined

The side and direction is what matters,
But I was not ready to understand
That Fortune is a fickle thing and not a subject to
my foolish demands

We called our little girl our Star
The card kept jumping out at us
Now, the only card I get is the fool
But not because I've been foolish
Because I'm at a new beginning

When I shuffle the cards,
Willing the universe to send me wisdom to make
sense of everything

How are you doing?

"How are you doing?" everyone asks

I wish the earth could open up and swallow me
    whole
I probably shouldn't have said that to my friends

People ask me what they can do to help
If there is any way to support

The only way they could help is to bring my baby
    back to me
But they can't do that.
I couldn't even keep her around

I couldn't even take the call and like a coward
    asked my wife to take it instead
Stupid me for thinking it would be good news

The news ripped through her like a bullet
Going clear through someone's heart

I want to believe everyone involved tried their
    best
I want to believe that I didn't jinx it when I got
the crib and diapers

I want to believe this isn't the fates cackling at
me for thinking I would get to build a nursery

And thinking my wife would be
A great stay-at-home mom

Or thinking I would be a good mom
Because I had a great example.

The doctors and nurses say they mourn with me
But I know for them it's just Tuesday

They can't know the depth of my pain
If they did, they would never come back to work

They shouldn't know

But that doesn't mean I can't stop it from leaking
        out when they ask what they can do

The pain overflows my cup like an ocean an
        iceberg melted into

The anger at whatever force stole her from my
womb consumes me like the pressure of a volcano

I want to rage and burn and destroy everything in
        my path
I wish the earth would open up and swallow me
        whole

My body is still here

But my mind is split in two

One side trying to stop the pain from turning to
        poison in my veins

The other debates let it swallow me whole.

The latter is never the side that wins the call to
    void

But I'm scared that's only because it hasn't
    gotten loud enough

The worst part—a contest

The worst part is knowing your next period is
emotionally a miscarriage.

Maybe it's wondering what's wrong with me
because everything on paper looked like it was
going to work so well.

But it didn't.

No, no. Here's the worst part; knowing there
must be something wrong with me. And then
the intrusive thoughts like maybe the universe
is telling me I shouldn't try again because I
shouldn't be a mother because the embryos were
perfect until they threw my body into the mix,
and then I think about all the fucking meditations
I did about trusting my body to do the one thing
I've ever asked it to do and how that all was a
fucking lie because my body clearly can't do the
one thing I want it to do. The one thing I've ever
really asked for and wanted so bad. Two years
of my life devoted to trying and for what? So the
universe could dangle this chance in my face,
then flip a coin and take it all away.

No, wait—I know what the worst part is.

The absolute worst part is knowing that this

happens to more families and women than just mine. Knowing it's so common that it just happens and there's nothing you can do about it. And even though I know all of this, the fact that they say it gets better the second time is enough to still make me want to try and put myself through all of this again so we can have a family of more than just two of us.

Hold on. I think I figured it out.

The worst part of it isn't losing the baby or thinking there's something wrong with my anatomy or knowing I'll put myself through all of this again. It's how once you talk about it you see how many people mourned their own losses in secret. Once you tell them, you seem like you're part of the world's worst members-only club. Why should we have to hide our pain in silence?

I will not let her be another story that turns to dust in my mind. The life she would have had with us will be celebrated every day. I just wish others would talk about it more so we didn't have to mourn in the dark.

Grief

Hope is a thing with feathers

The grief comes in waves

It ebbs and flows

I'll throw my energy into work

Into the chores and the drama of life

I'll do it to lose myself and the pain too

And I'll work hard on all my other dreams

to forget how badly I want to hear your laugh

I'm sorry to keep you waiting, little one.

Who knew timing would be so hard?

But you'll be fine and here with us soon

And knowing that helps heal my heart

Shock

I've never failed a test in my life,

and I won't start now with one that's so
      important

A negative is a failure as far as I'm concerned,
      and I don't ever fail

And I can't fail my daughter

Not when we had started picking out names for
      her

Not when the nursery is just starting to look like
      it's ready for her

Not when our friends were so excited we get to go
      through this with them together

So the doctor must be wrong.

Denial

Who cares what the doctor says
I refused to let this give me nightmares
The doctors were probably talking about someone
	else
Did I scare you away? Did I want you too bad?
I must have missed a step because I swore we had
		Infinite time
You, Mom, and me
We were supposed to be a family
I'd make any trade to get you back
I'd lie and cheat
To have you on your way again
But I know any of these bargains are just pretend.

Anger

The stupidest thing I've ever done is think I could
    trust my body
This body has given me so many reasons to fear
myself and my own cells within
The panics from things that could never kill me
The sadness deep in my soul makes my body too
    heavy
I cannot bring myself to stand up tall
I can only lie and lean
There is nothing here to prop me up
Because I must let go of my shattered dream

Bargaining

Last time I bargained
I begged
And pleaded
But it didn't work
So instead I let my mind wonder
And my imagination wander
To suppose another world where I could find her
again and bring her home
I wish I could go to the underworld
But not for the reason you think
Lately, I've been fascinated by the tale
Of Orpheus and Eurydice
The fates that followed her
Seemed destined

Acceptance, maybe?

The last step in the grieving process is acceptance,

so I guess I should think about it.

No.

I will not accept.

I will not lie down and take this beating life is
giving me.

They must have confused me with someone else.

I am not the one to wave the flag of surrender.

I am the one who will wage war and go to battle

against those who expect less of me.

Depression

Did I jinx what I tried to manifest?
Is this my fault because I bought that crib?
Was wishful thinking just the thing
to tempt the fates and foil my dreams?
Is there something wrong that I didn't know?
Was there something more I should have said?
Maybe my body's revolting because I didn't give
        it something.
So it decided to take away
The greatest gift, all I've wanted.
For three years now I've been begging but now
        I'm just haunted.
My little infinity, my little star,
My heart is shattered with you gone, so far away.

Strength

I don't think I am human, I'm too strong to be
There must be a reason why these forces like to
     pile these hardships on me
I don't think I am human—others are too easy to
     break
But I am exhausted by the way they gawk at all
     my strength
They think you don't have feelings when you
     brush off a nasty fall
They marvel at how you pick yourself off–
     forgetting the pain from the freefall

Oh how I wish to be human and stop being held
     up so high
The agony and wailing, and yet people still act
     surprised
It should have killed me they must suppose, And
     yet I'm still alive

Feeling the pain isn't shameful, And hiding it
     should never be the goal
But I'm not special, I'm just lucky I've never had
     to walk alone
To have friends who lift me when I all but
     disappear
And family that won't go away so I know they're
     always here.
When it hurts too much, they check in and I know
     they'll always stay
And when I have no more strength, they lend me
     theirs till I'm okay.

Acceptance, take two

I'm still convinced everything was fine until
something ripped you from me and something
happened and I had no way to see

My acceptance comes from admitting that not
knowing will keep me free

Free from blaming myself if falling from balance is
what took you from me

Free of crimes to the underworld once Hades heard
my plea

Because I'd say anything if it would make the fate
give me your key

I'd take you away, my little love, and our family
would flee

But I accept that sometimes knowing is worse than
uncertainty

Because if I knew it was somehow my fault, it
would always punish me

So in a way, I accept that this, that we, will never be

And the light from your star will guide me while I
am out to sea

Recovery again?

I knew the mental recovery would be difficult
but the physical one is almost worse.
Red tides rage through my body
And rips you from me

The mental wounds I thought I'd patched up
Become unstitched and tear me open
Depression grays the rest of the world around me
Tears fall from my eyes to drown me in this endless
sad

I was ready with my heart in my hands
Three swords impaled it as I became their prey
Hormones push and pull me
I feel lost at sea in my own mind.

One minute I feel normal,
then I can't walk because

my hips are being forced back into their usual form
after being pulled apart weeks before

Moving books into boxes makes me dizzy and taking
paintings off the wall makes me feel faint.
It wasn't just a lie I was telling myself.
It was happening and then un–happening.

I need another Xanax.
I don't know if knowing and waiting to lose her makes
it worse or better than
if she had just been ripped away.

Part of me wishes they had let me
Live with the lie so I could feel alive again,
but I know the shock from not knowing
Would destroy me more.

I wish they could have given me more time with her.
I loved her for only a fortnight,
and I loved her so much
It's ruining my life

How can others do this so many times

when the missed try hurts so bad at first?

Is this pain that burns in my chest

Ever going to go away?

I keep thinking it will feel better the next day,

but then I wake up and live it all over again

I couldn't get out of bed for the first full day after the

news because I kept sobbing.

We had to cancel plans with friends because going out

and having coffee with them is too hard.

We can't talk about other things when our friends say,

"Not again."

No one talks about how much grief will pile on.

Numbness

Feelings are so inconvenient

I wish I'd been turned to stone

Then I'd let these feelings wash away

The waves would erode the sadness

Maybe they'll clear away the pain

Or maybe it will take me away too

Denial, again

How far away are the stars really?

Just a few thousands of hundreds of miles?

That shouldn't be too bad a walk

Or maybe a road trip would be better

If we find enough good songs for our Playlist,

it will feel like no time has passed by the time we
    get there.

Haunted

I have unfinished business with you.
Please don't leave me yet!
There are so many things I want to tell you
Before our sun must set
Fake memories of the life we would have
collect a celestial debt

Vivid colorful dreams of who I wondered you'd be
have turned into a monochrome blue
These walls I thought you would play within,
this puzzle I hoped we would do.
These cushions I got so it would be easier
to lie down and play with you

The ghost of you will never leave me
Even if a future rainbow finds us
I won't give up on growing our family
So, my little angel, your memory won't turn to dust

Acceptance, for real this time

Acceptance, for real this time

I think I found you on the astral plane

Or maybe it was just my imagination

But it gave me closure all the same

When I cried into my pillow a sad declaration

"I want my baby back with me" and then I said
    your name

You found your way into my arms and I felt
    jubilation

My Hermit self, withdrawing, gave into an unjust
    shame

But you found me in my lonely contemplation

Our past and future now feels like a game

Or a joke of my attempted manifestation

But you were beyond all my earthly pain

Your little self, carried like a queen became my
    comforting inspiration

Through the joy of holding you, my pain
    escaped—almost unseen

Through this strange celestial space, I also heard

your voice

It sounded somewhere in between your mom's
voice and the voice of me

I said I was sorry you couldn't stay with us, you
told me you didn't want to leave

The Wheel of Fortune cycles on, and changes
things in an instant

But it wasn't up to any of us to let you go so
unexpectedly

I ask that when you have a break from being a
distant star

You come back to us now and then to remind us
you aren't that far

We'll love you every single day, and sing a lullaby
while we're apart

We said our I love yous and I came back to myself
again

Renewed by hearing your voice and laugh

The emotions raging in my soul finally laid to rest

My little star was out in the world, doing what
she had to do

So I'll keep a candle going, so you can visit us
again soon

IN HER HONOR

48

Down the rabbit hole

Your mom and me, hand in hand

Journeyed into Wonderland

With test tubes and doctors and catheters and
    scrubs for us two

We thought we caught you and could bring you
    home

But you went through the looking glass instead

I'll fill a jar full of stars so I can hold you

Your mom will immortalize you in her art

We'll both tattoo you on our shoulders

So we won't have to stay apart

For her

Did you know a tattoo doesn't hurt half as much
    as injections for egg retrieval?
Two times in the evening and then, after a week,
    a third at dawn
This memory tattoo wasn't even as close to the
    pain of the catheters up my cervix from the
    transfer
And that doesn't hurt as much as all the tests and
    transfers
And it's nothing compared to the pain of losing
    your baby in your mind, in your body
    back-to-back
This ink is a beautiful way to honor how you
    always carry them with you
Even if you weren't able to carry them into the
    world
The tattoo can be the colors they would have
    painted your days
My wife chose a peaceful, cheerful yellow for the
    star
Who would have brightened our days
I chose blue like the nighttime sky
when the stars are out to shine

Impatience

I didn't think it was possible to miss
someone I never fully got to know

And I think of things that I should say to you
But I know that I will never be able to say them
        out loud

Because I'm afraid that how I feel is what drove
        you away
And I don't want to keep knowing
what life is like without you here

This poem was originally a love song
But now it's an ode to all I lost

From the one test, I can't seem to ever pass
So all things unsaid will stay between us

The flame

I know it's just a symbol
We lit the candles to say goodbye
The candle was just a metaphor
Like the jar of stars, we painted with your name
The flame we kept going for a week as we said
        our goodbyes
Is no different than the tattoos on our shoulders
Or the Sigil in the Shadows book
The candle doesn't mean you didn't have to go
Just like taller buildings don't bring you any
        closer to a God
But still
We don't want the candle to go out

The Celestial Process

Is this how forlorn Demeter felt

When a man stole her daughter away to the
    underworld?

Then made her daughter parade around as
    goddess of spring when they deigned to let
    her be free?

A pain so raw and intense I could turn the earth
    cold

Kill the harvest and let the innocents starve from
    the ice encased around my heart

Is this the rage Brigid knew—

When she was born from flames?

When they killed her child in battle

How she felt them draw their last breath

Knowing she could have saved them if she only
    had more time?

A rage that burns too intense, you go blind if you
    look too long

It could burn the tower to the ground

The flames reaching toward the heavens

Like when she came to the world in a blaze of fire
and forged the sacred flame?

The sacred flame melts the winter I have made
for myself

I become reborn from the new waters washing
over me.

The tower is reborn

The world finds its temperance again

And with our three cups full once more

We, mothers, are unbreakable

And together we find serenity

Demeter finds me in my sadness

and helps me keep my cool

Brigid warmed my heart again

And the king of kings, the lord of lords,

reminded me I'm not alone in this

With all their love forever more.

Wondering

Would you be beautiful and pale with golden hair
    like me?
Would you have the same love to laugh, dance,
    and sing—
Angela Amanda?

Would you take comfort in the stories you and I
    would weave-
And would we craft a life like a breathtaking
    tapestry?
My little lightseer, thank you for choosing me.
We would have worked together as mommy and
    my sweet baby—
Angela Amanda.

Or would you have copper hair and eyes full of
    dreams?
Like your mom, would you see The Best in every
    little thing?
Would you fill the world with essays and tell all
    the truth Slant
And would you make each day an adventure or a
    quest—
Angela Amanda?

Sweet dreams, my daughter, all is well, we all will
    find—
You're always with us, our star, you're still mine.
I'll miss and think of you until the day I die
But grief sweeps me away less as each hour goes
    by—
Angela Amanda

The Star

By Dewy

You may be light-years away
but I can still feel your glow.
We may not meet physically
but your love I do know.

May your existence be blessed
wherever you happen to be.
I'll be sure to come find you
once my soul escapes my body.

Whichever afterlife you've adopted,
I will find my way around.
Assuming you want to see me,
I know you will be found.

There is nothing that can stop me;
I care not what the gods allow.
In the meantime, I'll stay here
cursed to remain apart for now.

My star

I know it's just a symbol
My little love, my little boo
It's so hard to say goodbye to you

My little star, shining so bright
You are all around tonight

And in the day, all hours, too
I hope you know I'll think of you

I felt you so strong the moment we met
And I'll hold you as long as the gods protect

Together we always have infinity
We'll keep you with us, your mom and me

So this is not a true goodbye
For my little star will always light up my sky

My world is yours, loved little one
So you go on and outshine the sun

Acknowledgments

First and foremost, I would like to express my deepest gratitude to my family. Your unwavering support, love, and encouragement have been the cornerstone of my creative journey. To my parents, for nurturing my love for literature and always believing in my dreams, thank you. Thank you to my entire care team at Spring Fertility. It was a rollercoaster of a journey, but you all were there to get me through it. Thank you to my therapist and psychiatrist, I literally wouldn't have been able to stop having panic attacks without you all.

A heartfelt thank you to my friends Alana, Dawn, Nicole, Holly, Kris, Mike, Natalie, and Mohan who have been with us throughout our journey. Your honest feedback and constant encouragement have been invaluable in the creation of this collection.

Special thanks to Mad Women Publishing and Sharon Skinner, my book coach, editor, formatter, and cover designer, for believing in my vision and for your meticulous editing and support throughout the publishing process. Your expertise and dedication have truly brought this book to life. I have literally no idea where this project would be without you.

And of course thank you to my amazing, strong, and beautiful wife, Dewy. You are always my lighthouse when I feel like I'm lost at sea.

Finally, to the readers—thank you for taking the time to explore my poetry. Your engagement and appreciation are the ultimate rewards of this creative endeavor.

With gratitude,
Colleen Griffith